Arts & Crafts

MODELING

Susie O'Reilly

With photographs by Zul Mukhida

Thomson Learning
New York

Titles in this series

BATIK AND TIE-DYE
BLOCK PRINTING
MODELING
PAPERMAKING
STENCILS AND SCREENS
WEAVING

Frontispiece *A model of modeling!*
This little figure, from Venezuela,
shows a woman making a coil pot.

First published in the
United States in 1993 by
Thomson Learning
115 Fifth Avenue
New York, NY 10003

First published in 1993 by
Wayland (Publishers) Ltd.

Cataloging-in-Publication Data applied for

ISBN: 1-56847-066-5

Printed in Italy

CONTENTS

Words printed in **bold** appear in the glossary.

GETTING STARTED

Many everyday things are made of clay: bricks and tiles for building houses; plates and cups; and pots for green plants.
Clay is also used by artists and craftspeople to make models, **sculptures**, and decorative objects. Objects made from clay are called "pottery."

Clay is a natural material that is dug out of the earth. Clay was formed many millions of years ago. Over hundreds of centuries, frost, wind, rain, and heat from the sun worked away at rocks on the earth's surface, wearing down some areas to tiny, sticky grains of clay. Clay can be many different colors, depending on the **minerals** contained in the original rocks. For example, clay with iron in it is reddish-brown or yellowish-orange.

▼ *This man is adding water to clay and pounding it with his feet to make it softer and easier to model.*

When clay is first dug out of the ground it is soft and wet, so it is easy to model. In the air, the water in the clay starts to **evaporate**. The clay dries out and becomes lighter in color. It can no longer be modeled. If the clay is then heated to a high temperature—in a bonfire or **kiln**—any water left is dried out of it and it changes again. It becomes extremely hard. This process is called **firing**.

Clay appears in these three different forms because it is made of flat, **hexagonal** shaped **particles**. When clay is wet, there is water between the particles, so they can slip and slide around. As the clay becomes drier, there is nothing for the particles to slide on. When the clay is heated, the particles **fuse** together.

There are three main ways of shaping clay: using a **potter's wheel**, a **mold** made of **plaster**, or your hands. This book looks at ways of shaping clay by hand. The same ideas can be used with other modeling materials: cold clays and modeling clay, which can be bought in stores, or homemade play dough and salt dough.

▲ *The ancient Greeks made models of everyday scenes. Try making your own, like this one.*

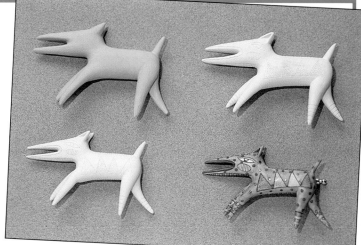

▲ *These pottery brooches show clay at four different stages: (top row) wet; dry but not fired; (bottom row) fired; decorated and fired again.*

TOOLS AND MATERIALS

To get started you will need the following equipment.

Materials
clay (bought or freshly dug); fine sand for adding to freshly dug clay; cold clay or modeling clay

General equipment
apron; wooden board (unvarnished) or piece of cotton cloth to work on; plastic wrap, plastic bags, and airtight containers; old toothbrush; old table knife; rolling pin; spray bottle; paper and pencils; graph paper

Modeling tools
popsicle sticks; old screwdriver; comb; etc.

Scraping and smoothing tools
sponge; seashells; wooden ruler or spoon; etc.

Decorating tools
plastic cutlery; pastry cutters; darning needle; nails; screws; buttons; leaves; twigs; pine cones; pebbles; string; bottle caps; sieve or garlic press; etc.

For making dough
flour; salt; powder paint; food coloring; cream of tartar; cooking oil; plastic bowl; baking tray

For finishing
poster paints; acrylic varnish; white glue

For cleaning up
scraper; broom; dustpan and brush; sponge

Safety Note
Be careful not to create clay dust—breathing it in can be harmful. Do not scrape dried clay with sandpaper. Clean up small pieces of clay using a damp cloth. Wipe work areas with a damp sponge. Avoid brushing as much as possible.

If you get clay on your clothing, wait for it to dry completely and then brush it off.

Do not wash clay down the sink. It will block the drain.

THE HISTORY OF MODELING

People have been cooking and storing food in clay pots for at least 8,000 years. Even 100,000 years before that, clay was being used to make models of people and animals. These models were probably meant to ward off evil spirits and bring good luck.

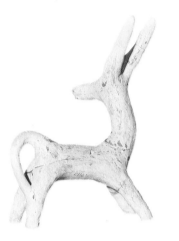

◀ *This animal figure is probably a deer. It was found on the Greek island of Crete and was made about 4,000 years ago.*

Among the early peoples of North and South America there were highly skilled potters. Archaeologists have found coiled, molded, and modeled pots, decorated with complex designs. For example, there are cooking pots decorated with modeled faces. The faces look upward, so they can be seen by people standing over the pot.

It seems that early people took great care when choosing and preparing their clay. Sometimes they would travel a great distance to collect special clay, or they would add sand or ash so that delicate figures could be modeled and fired without the clay cracking.

Clay objects provide useful information about the world's earliest peoples. Clay that has been fired may shatter, but it does not rot away like wood or fabric, so **archaeologists** have been able to piece together broken pottery. Many clay objects have been found in ancient graves. People were often buried with cooking pots, jewelry, toys, and other items. They thought they might need them in their next life.

◀ *A Peruvian pot, with a handle and spout, made in the shape of a jaguar (a big cat). It is over 1,000 years old.*

A model of a man kneeling, made in Japan in the seventh century. ▶

The ancient Egyptians, Greeks, and Romans made clay models of everyday scenes. For example, there are models of people taking baths, going to market, playing musical instruments, and acting in plays. These models were often made as toys or perfume bottles.

This ancient ▶ bowl comes from what is now Egypt. The inside has been rubbed to make it shiny.

▲ *A scene from everyday life: this ancient Greek model shows a man sawing wood.*

▼ *An army of life-size soldiers, guarding an ancient tomb in Xian, China.*

Throughout history, the Chinese have been famous for their pottery skills. A lot of early Chinese pottery has been found in **tombs**. During times of war, whole armies of soldiers, sometimes life-size, were modeled, painted in bright colors, and buried in the tombs of important people. It was believed that they would protect the dead from their enemies.

▼ *In Nigeria, Africa, over 2,000 years ago, people made models of human heads.*

MODERN MODELING

In some parts of the world, for example in South America and Africa, people still make pottery using the same coiling, molding, and modeling techniques used by their **ancestors** hundreds, or even thousands, of years ago.

▲ *American potter Richard Zane Smith uses extremely thin coils to build large pots. He leaves the coils showing as part of the design.*

◀ *In Mexico, even large pots are made by hand.*

▼ *A potter from Tanzania, East Africa, smooths the surface of a hand-modeled pot.*

In **developed countries**, most clay goods—pipes, bricks, tiles, and crockery—are made in factories. In the eighteenth and nineteenth centuries, the **Industrial Revolution** brought great changes to western Europe and the United States. Huge machines and factories were built to produce cheap goods in large amounts. It seemed that potters who worked by hand were no longer needed.

In the twentieth century, however, artists and craftspeople have again become interested in hand-modeled pottery. They have studied hand-modeling techniques from around the world. In many developed countries, especially England, Japan, the United States, and Canada, young people train in college to work with clay. Craftspeople are able to earn a living from their work, making sculptures and pots.

A pot by ▶ Bernard Leach, a famous English potter. Leach went to live in Japan in 1909, and learned how the Japanese made pots. Many European potters were influenced by his work.

Clay can be ▶ modeled to make jewelry. This teapot earing was made by Californian Jaye Lawrence.

Many modern potters use a wheel, but others hand-build, using a mixture of pinching, coiling, and slabbing techniques. Although they are using the same methods potters have used for thousands of years, they also make full use of all the technical and scientific information available today. They are very fussy about the clay they use. They search carefully to find clay that will do just what they want.

◀ *This clown brooch was hand-made by Trish Rafferty.*

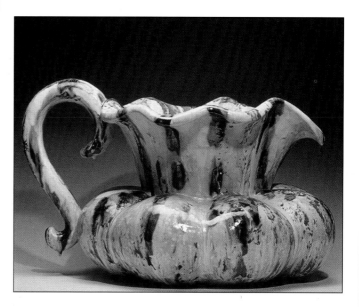

Kate Malone takes ideas from nature for her ▶ work. Does this jug remind you of a pumpkin?

PREPARING THE CLAY

Clay can be bought at arts and crafts stores. That modeling clay usually comes in two colors. Red clay gets its color from the iron it contains. It is warm and earthy but can stain hands and equipment. Gray clay does not stain, but it leaves more dust. It is easier to paint.

Store-bought modeling clay sometimes has pieces of fired clay or sawdust added to it. This gives it more body and makes it easier to work with. It also helps the clay hold any shape it is modeled into.

If your home was a yard with clay soil, you may be able to dig your own clay. Never do this without asking an adult first. Both bought and fresh-dug clays need to be prepared before you can start modeling.

PREPARING STORE-BOUGHT CLAY

1 The clay is sold in a plastic bag. Before you start, check its **consistency**. It should not be too dry or too wet. Roll a piece of the clay into a small ball with your hands and squeeze it with your fingers. It should feel soft and stay in the shape you squeeze.

◀ *Three types of common clay: (from left) gray; red; with fired clay added.*

2 If the clay cracks easily, it is too dry. Shape it into balls the size of your fist. Push your thumbs into the center of the balls. Fill them with water and put them in a plastic bag for a day or two. The clay will absorb the water and become soft enough to model.

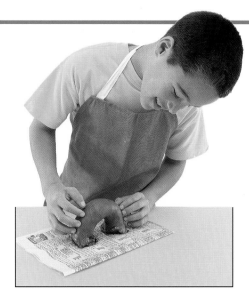

its ends, and leave it for a day. The air will dry out the clay.

4 Clay is usually full of air bubbles. If it is heated in a kiln, the air bubbles will **expand** and shatter the clay. **Kneading** the clay gets rid of the air bubbles, and also makes it easier to model.

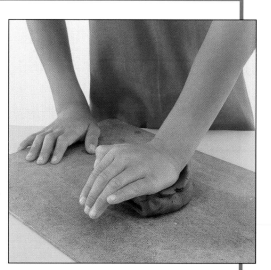

3 If the clay sticks to your fingers, it is too wet. Roll it into a thick sausage. Bend it over so that it stands on

Put a lump of clay on an unvarnished board or some cotton cloth (to keep it from sticking to the table). Use

the heel of your palm to keep pushing the clay away from you. It helps to stand as you do this.

PREPARING FRESHLY DUG CLAY

1 Ask an adult to help you find an area of clay soil and dig up a clump of it.

2 Pick out all the stones, twigs, and leaves in the clay.

Remember: Clay, cold clay, play dough, and salt dough all dry out quickly. If you want to reuse clay or dough, or to continue working on a model at another time, wrap it in plastic wrap or put it in an airtight container.

3 If it is sticky, mix in some fine sand. You will need about two parts of sand to three parts of clay. This will make it easier to model and help it keep its shape.

4 Now knead the clay as you would if it were store-bought.

PINCHING

The simplest way to start modeling is by pinching, pulling, and squeezing. You can use clay, salt dough, play dough, modeling compound, or cold clays. Make models of animals, people, or plants. Or make all kinds of pots—broad and low, tall and thin, large, small, bulky, or delicate. It's up to you!

MAKING A MODEL

▼ *Try making models using modeling clay of various colors.*

1 Take a piece of clay or dough. With your hands, start to pinch and squeeze the lump into the shape of a bird, an animal, a person, or a plant.

2 As you pull and push the clay or dough, it may begin to suggest a new shape to you. Help this new idea along. Give the shape more features by adding extra pieces.

3 Try using some of your modeling tools to add details and decoration.

MAKING PINCH POTS

1 Take a lump of clay that fits into the palm of your hand. Roll it into a smooth ball between your palms.

2 Hold the lump in one hand and press the thumb of your other hand into the middle of the ball, making a deep hole.

3 Keep the ball cupped in your hand and pinch out the clay between your thumb and fingers. Keep turning the ball of clay

around in your hand, and carefully pull out the walls. Slowly pinch them out so that they become thinner and thinner.

4 After a while the walls will become floppy. Put the pot to one side, standing it upside down on its rim. Leave it for about an hour.

5 When the clay has stiffened, continue pinching out the shape.

VARIATIONS

1 Add a coil to the top to make a rim. Pinch out the rim to make it look like the edge of a pie.

2 Add a coil to the bottom of the pot to make a base. See pages 14-15 for instructions on making coils.

3 You can also model feet to add to the base of the pot.

MAKING COIL POTS

Using coils of clay is one way to build up shapes, layer by layer. The shape grows gradually, so you can think carefully about how it looks as you go along—and make changes if you wish.
Tiny pots and huge pots, even pots as big as a person, can be made with coils. In Nigeria, West Africa, potters use clay coils to build houses!

1 Break off a piece of clay. Roll it between your hands to make a sausage shape.

2 Place the sausage on a wooden board and roll it using both of your hands. Keep rolling until it is about as fat as a felt-tipped pen. Make about six rolls, all the same thickness.

3 Roll out a piece of clay with a rolling pin. Use a lid from a jar or tin can to cut out the base for a pot.

4 Place a coil on the base, running it around the outside edge. Smooth it firmly to the base on the inside, using your thumb or a modeling tool.

5 When you have worked all around the base, break off any extra coil. Use your fingers to smooth the ends together.

6 Now add a second coil on top of the first one. As you add coils, make sure you place the ends in different places. Support the wall of the pot with one hand and smooth the inside with the fingers of your other hand.

TURN TO PAGE 5 FOR A LIST OF TOOLS TO USE

7 To make the pot get fatter, place each coil on the outside edge of the one before. To make it get thinner, place each coil on the inside edge.

8 Once you are pleased with the size and shape of the pot, smooth over all the outside coils. Use the tools you have collected to beat, scrape, or smooth the pot.

VARIATIONS

1 To get a really smooth surface, let the pot dry until it is damp. Then rub it with the back of a metal spoon or a round pebble. This is called **burnishing**.

2 Pinch and squeeze the clay on the side of the pot to make a raised pattern. Add pieces of clay or modeled figures.

3 Use some of your decorating tools to press a pattern into the clay. Or leave the coils showing on the outside as a decorative feature.

MAKING SLAB POTS

Slabs are used to make straight-sided pots and models. You can make containers or model houses, boats, and bridges. If you are making a very regular shape, it helps to make a paper **template** to use as a pattern from which the parts can be cut. Slabs can also be made into attractive tiles. You can scratch a pattern or design into the surface, or add pieces of clay to make a raised decoration.

USING FIRM CLAY

◄ *Try using slabs to make model buildings out of modeling clay*

3 Put your templates on the clay and cut out the shapes, using a knife.

1 Decide what you are going to make—perhaps a box or a model house—and work out the **measurements** for the slabs you will need. On graph paper, make templates for the pieces.

2 Using a rolling pin, roll a piece of clay flat on a board or piece of cotton cloth. To get an even surface, roll the clay between two strips of wood, about half an inch thick.

4 Roughen the edges of the slabs, so that they grip each other firmly when they are joined.

5 If you are using clay, wet the edges with a brush so that they become sticky. If you are using modeling clay or play dough, you do not need to dampen the edges.

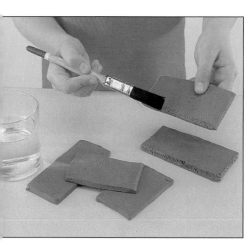

Using Soft Clay

1 Roll out a sheet of clay on a piece of cloth. Wrap it around a tube—perhaps an old plastic bottle, or the tube from a roll of paper towels.

6 Join the pieces together, smoothing the seams firmly with your fingers.

4 Cut out a base from another slab. Roughen and dampen the edges. Join the base to the tube.

5 Change the shape of the pot—pinch the sides or add extra clay. Try cutting away pieces of the pot to make a pattern of holes.

2 Cut the clay so that the edges meet and smooth over the seam.

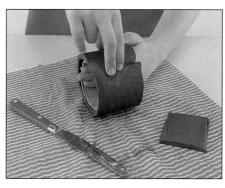

7 For extra strength, roll out very thin ropes of clay and press them into each join, on the inside.

3 Allow the clay to stiffen, then remove the tube.

SALT DOUGH

Salt dough is easy to make. Salt dough models will last for many years if they are properly dried and varnished. **Remember: salt dough may look like cookie dough, but it cannot be eaten**.

MAKING SALT DOUGH

You will need:

$^1/_3$ cup of flour
$^2/_3$ cup of salt
$^1/_3$ cup of water
3 teaspoons of powder paint, any color

1 Mix together the salt, flour, and powder paint in an old plastic or glass bowl.

2 Add water to the mixture and stir well to make a firm dough.

3 Knead the dough, using the heel of your palm (see page 11). This will mix the ingredients together thoroughly.

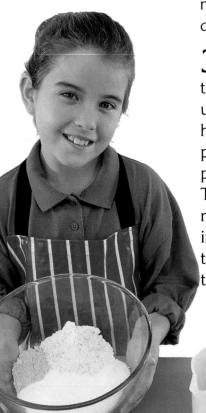

4 Put the dough in a plastic bag, tie up the top, and leave it overnight in the refrigerator.

5 Use other powder paints to make doughs in different colors.

5 To stick on the decorations, dampen the backs using a brush that has been dipped in water.

MAKING TREE ORNAMENTS

1 Make templates of shapes to cut around. Try stars, boots, faces, birds, airplanes, or anything you like.

2 Take your dough out of the refrigerator. Put some flour on a wooden board (so that the dough does not stick) and roll out the dough with a rolling pin.

3 Put the templates on the dough and cut around them with a knife.

4 Decorate your shapes with pieces of dough of different colors. To do this, roll out a thin slab of dough. Press out small shapes using cookie cutters or bottle caps. Experiment and have fun.

6 Make a small hole at the top of each shape, so that when they are done, you can thread some string through to hang them up.

7 Put the shapes on a baking tray. Ask an adult to put the tray in an oven set at 350 degrees. Bake for 30 minutes. When they are cool and dry, use acrylic varnish, first on one side and then the other.

PLAY DOUGH

Play dough can be poked, squeezed, rolled into slabs, and coiled like clay. If you keep it in an airtight container, the same dough can be used over and over.

MAKING PLAY DOUGH

1 Measure the ingredients carefully, and mix them together in a bowl.

2 Put the mixture in a saucepan and heat on a burner at a low setting. **Ask an adult to help you do this**. Keep stirring until the mixture turns into a ball. Turn off the heat.

3 When the dough is cool, knead it thoroughly (see page 11).

4 Make dough in a variety of colors.

You will need:

²/₃ cup of flour
¹/₄ cup of salt
¹/₂ cup of water

1 tablespoon of cooking oil
3 teaspoons of cream of tartar
1 teaspoon of food coloring or powder paint

PLAY DOUGH MODELS

1 Make a living room scene. Roll out a slab of play dough. Add play dough in other colors to make a patterned rug.

2 Pinch out the body and head of a cat. Stick on extra play dough for the tail and feet.

3 Use play dough in different colors to model a person in an armchair.

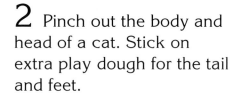

Think of other scenes to model; a circus, a fair, a visit to the zoo, an afternoon at the beach, or a football game. Ask some friends to work with you.

MODELING A PORTRAIT HEAD

Look carefully at people's heads. Make big, bold drawings of several people, using a soft pencil. Notice that each person's head has a different shape. The features—eyes, nose, lips, ears, hair—and the way they fit together vary from person to person. Make drawings of the back, front, and profile of one person's head. Try closing your eyes and gently feeling a friend's face.

1 Cut off a large piece of clay that is soft but not sticky. Put it on a board.

2 Model the clay into the basic shape of the head, neck, and shoulders.

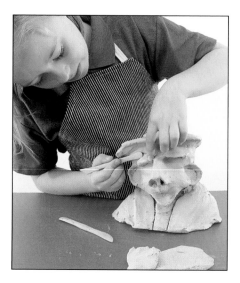

3 Pull, pinch, and squeeze out the eyes, eyebrows, ears, nose, and lips. Add extra pieces of clay if necessary.

4 Remember that your model is **three-dimensional**. Turn the head around to work on the sides and the back. Really good models are as interesting from the back and side as from the front.

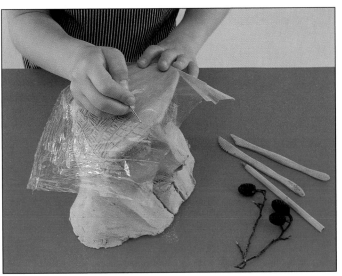

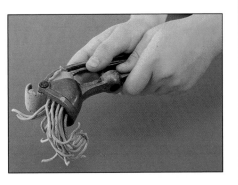

7 To make hair, press some clay through a sieve or a garlic press.

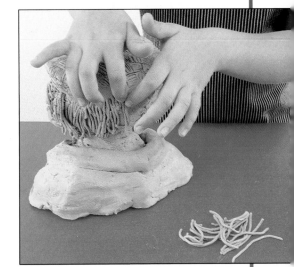

5 To model fine details, put a piece of plastic wrap over the area and use the end of a sewing needle to press or draw in the marks you want.

8 When you are pleased with your model, leave the head out to dry for a day. Then scratch in some fine details such as wrinkles around the eyes.

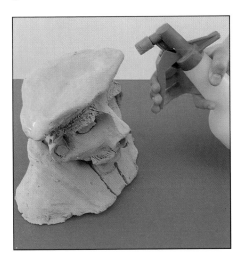

TURN TO PAGES **26-27** FOR IDEAS ON FINISHING YOUR MODEL.

6 If the clay begins to dry out, spray water on it using a spray bottle (the type used to spray houseplants). If you need to stop working, cover the clay carefully with plastic wrap to keep it from drying out.

MAKING A WALL PLAQUE

When you have learned the basic methods of modeling there is no end
to the things you can make. Invent ways of combining different methods.
Let your imagination go wild. Use your eyes, a notebook, or a camera
to look for things that give you ideas. The idea for this wall plaque
is a rock pool, but you could create something quite different.
For example, you could make a plaque to illustrate a story or tell
about things you like to do with your friends.

1 Roll out a slab of clay
and cut it into the shape you
want. Since this plaque is
about a rock pool, you could
choose the
shape of a crab
or a starfish.

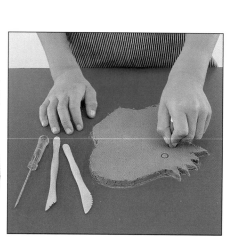

2 Make two holes in the
top of the plaque so that
you can attach string to
hang it on a wall.

3 Make other shapes and
stick them to the base slab.
Decide whether you want
them to lie flat on the base,
or stick out.

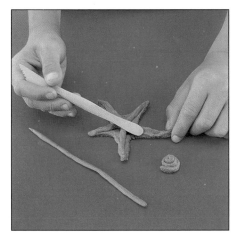

4 Make balls, rolls, and coils of clay to add to the basic shapes. Use your tools to press patterns into the clay. To make sure the clay dries out evenly, do not let any parts get too thick. This is especially important if you are going to fire it.

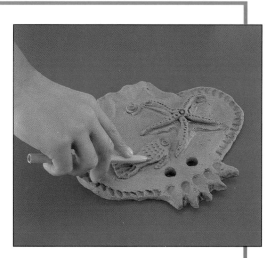

5 When you have finished modeling, allow your plaque to dry. Then decorate it with paint and acrylic varnish.

6 Thread a piece of ribbon or string through the holes at the top of the plaque to hang it on the wall.

TURN TO PAGES 26-27 FOR INFORMATION ON FINISHING AND DECORATING.

FINISHING AND DECORATING

Sometimes you may just have fun modeling, reusing the same clay or dough over and over. Sometimes, however, you may want to keep what you make. There are a number of ways to do this.

Clay can be fired in a kiln and then decorated with **glazes**. This involves special equipment, and you would need an adult to help you. There are other ways to finish clay that you can do yourself.

Salt dough and cold clays can be dried out thoroughly in a warm oven (half an hour at about 350 degrees). **Ask an adult to help you do this**. When the pieces are dry they can be painted and varnished. Some cold clays come in bright colors and do not need to be painted.

▲ *This plant stand has been fired but not glazed.*

This model ▶ rock pool was fired, decorated with colored glazes, and fired again.

PAINTING AND VARNISHING CLAY MODELS

1 Let the clay dry out completely. This will take several days.

2 Add water to white glue and paint this mixture all over the model. This will help to make the dry clay less crumbly and fragile.

4 Paint a basic color all over the model. Then add details in different colors. Use poster paints that are thick enough to use on top of each other, without the colors showing through.

5 When it is dry give the model two coats of acrylic varnish to protect it.

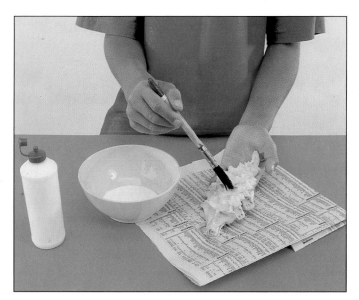

3 Paint the model with a coat of white paint for a good background to work on.

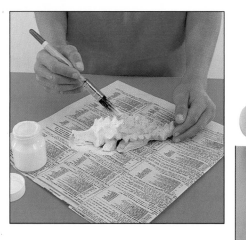

THE GALLERY

It is important to remember that models have three dimensions. This means that the things you make will be viewed from the front, the sides, and the back. When you are looking for ideas for modeling, try to find things that also have three dimensions.

Try drawing objects from different viewpoints. With a big sheet of paper and a soft pencil, make several big, bold drawings of the same object. If you discover that the back and the side view are uninteresting, choose something else to model.

▲ *Smooth pebbles.*

Close your eyes and handle some shells, stones, or pieces of pottery. You will be surprised at the range of different feelings you can get from the surface of an object. Think of words that describe the **textures**: rough, smooth, grainy, crumbly, spiky. These pictures will give you some ideas for things to look out for.

◄ *A carved creature from the front of a Viking ship, made in about A.D. 800.*

A starfish. ▶

▲ A sitting horse.

◀ A sculpture by Henry Moore.

▼ Rugged mountains that look like a monster's back.

◀ A prickly cactus.

▶ A pet cat.

▼ Round pumpkins.

Glossary

Ancestors Members of a family who lived long ago.

Archaeologists People who find out what happened in the past by studying ancient remains.

Burnishing Polishing a surface by rubbing it to make it extremely smooth.

Consistency The thickness or firmness of something.

Developed countries Countries that have complicated systems for industry, transportation, and finance. In *developing* countries, people rely on small-scale farming and crafts.

Evaporate To turn into a gas, like steam.

Expand To get bigger.

Firing Heating clay in a very hot oven, called a kiln, to make it extremely hard.

Fuse To join together by heating to a very high temperature; to melt together.

Glaze A shiny, glassy coating put on pottery to decorate and protect it. Glazes come in many different colors.

Hexagonal Six-sided.

Industrial Revolution The changes that took place in western Europe and the United States during the eighteenth and nineteenth centuries. Huge factories were built to produce goods in large amounts. Many people stopped working on farms and went to work at the new factories in towns instead.

Kiln A hot oven used for heating clay to a very high temperature.

Kneading Working a mixture into a dough or paste by pressing and squeezing it.

Measurements The exact size of an object.

Minerals Chemicals, such as copper and iron, that are found in rocks.

Mold A hollow case into which a liquid, such as plaster, can be poured. When the plaster sets, it takes on the shape of the mold.

Particles The smallest specks of a substance.

Plaster A white substance that is soft when wet, but that becomes very hard when it dries.

Potter's wheel A turntable that spins around. A potter puts a lump of soft clay in the middle and models the shape with his or her hands.

Sculpture A work of art made by carving or modeling.

Template A shape cut out of cardboard or paper. Templates are used to produce the same shape accurately several times.

Texture The feel of the surface of an object.

Three-dimensional Having depth as well as height and width.

Tomb A room, usually below ground, in which a person is buried.

Further Information

Books to Read

Greenberg, Jan and Sandra Jordan. *The Sculptor's Eye: Looking at Contemporary American Art* (New York: Delacorte Press, 1993).

Hull, Jeannie. *Clay* (New York: Franklin Watts, 1989).

Pekarik, Andrew. *Behind the Scenes: Sculpture* (New York: Hyperion, 1992).

Potter, Tony. *An Usborne Guide to Pottery From Start to Finish.* (London: Usborne, 1985).

Schäl, Hannelore, Ulla Abdalla, & Angela Wiesner. *Toys Made of Clay.* (Chicago: Childrens Press, 1989).

Suppliers

Some suppliers of materials for modeling are listed below. Also check the Yellow Pages in the telephone directory.

American Art Clay Co., Inc.
4717 West 16th Street
Indianapolis, IN 46222

Byrne Ceramics
95 Bartley Road
Flanders, NJ 07836

Minnesota Clay
8001 Grand Avenue South
Bloomington, MN 55420

Westwood Ceramic Supply
14400 Lomitas Avenue
City of Industry, CA 91716

For further information about arts and crafts, contact the following organization:

American Craft Council
72 Spring Street
New York, NY 10012

INDEX

ACKNOWLEDGMENTS

The publishers would like to thank the following for allowing their photographs to be reproduced: Bridgeman Art Library 29 top left; Crafts Council 9 top right, 9 bottom right; C. M. Dixon 6 top and center, 7 top left; Eye Ubiquitous 5 right (P. Seheult), 8 left (E. Hawkins), 9 left, 29 top right (P. Seheult), 29 center right (C. Gibb); Gallery 10, Scottsdale and Santa Fe, 8 top right;

Michael Holford 7 bottom left, 28 left; Hutchison Library 8 bottom right (S. Errington); Tony Stone Worldwide 7 bottom right (J. Calder), 28 bottom right (D. Torckler); Werner Forman Archive 6 bottom, 7 top right; Zefa title page, 4, 28 top right, 29 center left, 29 bottom left, 29 bottom right. All other photographs, including cover, were supplied by Zul Mukhida. Logo artwork by John Yates.

The work by Henry Moore, Reclining Figure, 1945, illustrated on page 29, has been reproduced by kind permission of the Henry Moore Foundation.

The publishers would like to thank William and Laura Green for allowing their work to appear in photographs on page 26. The pieces were made during a workshop run by the Crafts Council.